THE SUCCCCCESS JOURNEY

The 5 Keys That Can Change Your Life

Kyle P. Marshall

Sermon To Book
www.sermontobook.com

The Succcccess Journey / Kyle P. Marshall
ISBN-13: 9780692361146
ISBN-10: 0692361146

This book is dedicated to the memory of my mother, Lillie Pearl Marshall.

She truly exemplified the love of Christ by the way she lived. Her love and devotion to her family, her church, her community and all who she came into contact with was unparalleled.

Also to my father, Walter L. Marshall, for being a living example of a man of valor who leads, provides, protects and loves his family! Thank you Daddy for being who you are in my life!

CONTENTS

5 Keys That Can Truly Change Your Life

With a house most would love, vehicles others envy, a 401K offering a great start for the family's retirement, real estate investments, a year or two from debt freedom (other than the mortgage), a beautiful wife, three wonderful children, a thriving ministry and a great corporate job—sounds great for a 30-something African-American man in America, right?

I went from married to divorced, from gainful employment to the unemployment line, from being on the road to financial freedom to financial ruin.

I thought so, too. But then in 2009, the house I built came tumbling down. Within a year, the real estate bubble burst, along with all hopes of any significant financial return; my 401K hit rock bottom and was split in half due to my divorce; the wife I was married to for 14 years was now on the other side of a divorce table, my kids who had only ever experienced a two-parent household were about to experience a broken home; my great corporate job that I enjoyed and netted a six-figure salary was now gone due to downsizing. If that wasn't enough, the house we enjoyed for years had plummeted in value.

> *And here's the amazing part: Up until 2009, outsiders looking in would have viewed my life as a success. I certainly considered it a success. I've learned that success cannot be defined by the standards most of us ascribe to.*

Get the picture? In a year's time, I went from married to divorced, from gainful employment to the unemployment line, from being on the road to financial freedom to financial ruin. I went from having a family "unit" to a divided, two-parent household for three children who had only known a unified family. The life that most would envy turned to the life that most would dread.

Up until 2009, outsiders looking in would have viewed my life as a success. I certainly did. But I've learned that success cannot be defined by the standards most of us ascribe to. Success is only defined from the joy of the journey that has been purposed *in* your life and *for* your life and *through* your life.

And here is the amazing part: after having "lost it all", I actually became more of a success without any of the things I possessed before. This book is a journey to help anyone who is searching for significance or success to truly know what it means to be successful while understanding the importance of the journey. I will challenge the notion that the "American Dream" can actually be a "Purposeful Disaster" — especially when you are not doing what you are destined to do.

Come along on this journey to discover 5 keys that can truly change your life and allow you to experience joy during the journey!

CHAPTER ONE

What Is Succcccess?

*Study this Book of Instruction continually. Meditate on it day and night so you will be sure to obey everything written in it. Only then will you prosper and succeed in all you do. — **Joshua 1:8***

Prior to 2009, I had defined success as the accumulation of cash, collateral, creature comforts and my credit score. The success could only be validated by how others viewed my accumulation of those things. Conceptually, I would provide lip service to success being much more than just what you have; however, in reality I equated or judged my own success based upon what I had. Once lost, it forced me to rethink what I had allowed my environment to influence me with.

Success is best defined, in my opinion, by first answering this question: What is God's plan for my life?

How Do You Define Success?

_____

_____

_____

_____

_____

_____

How you think about and look at your life's scenarios, situations, and challenges can actually be what you need to redefine your path to success. For some, success is defined by the accumulation of what you acquire, while others define success by the world's standards—lights, camera, action. After all, the people who get all the attention must be successful since they make so much money ... like movie stars, professional athletes, or public figures. If not them, then the individuals that you read about in the Wall Street Journal, Fortune or Black Enterprise, or any of the magazines that highlight people who have done well in their respective fields of study, work and interest. After all, they have the position, power, and prominent persona; thus, they must be successful. Or are they?

Independent of God's plan and purpose for your life, any "success" will be temporary, fleeting and unfulfilling.

If you define success straight by the book, then you'll be interested to know that Webster's Dictionary defines success this way: *outcome; result; degree or measure of succeeding or favorable or desired outcome; also, attainment of wealth, favor or eminence; one who succeeds.* Eminence, as defined by Webster's, means a position of prominence or superiority. The beauty of these definitions is that they all point toward something good. At a very elementary level, success seems like it could never be a bad thing. Results, desired outcome, attainment of wealth, prominence, or even superiority— those can't be bad. Or can they?

Success is best defined, in my opinion, by first answering this question: What is God's plan for my life? As Rick Warren says, "What on earth am I here for?" In other words, what is my God- given purpose? Once that question is pondered and answered, then the pursuit of that purpose or plan becomes the degree of your success.

This success may not look like the world's success and—unlike the world's success—it will bring contentment and a degree of satisfaction.

It has less to do with your accumulation of wealth, although it may come as a result of it. The book of John suggests that your love for God, followed by obedience, produces fruit. Fruit for some may be different than for others. Would the woman with 2 mites be "successful" in today's society? I'm not sure, but the fact that she was obedient to the plan for her life makes her an over-whelming success!

Contentment doesn't breed compla-cency but it does provide joy on your journey to continue to go to another level.

Independent of God's plan and purpose for your life, any "success" will be temporary, fleeting and unful-filling. However, when directed by God's plan and purpose for your life, not only will any success be lasting but it will also be sustainable and fulfilling.

This success may not look like the world's success and—unlike the world's success—it will bring content-ment and a degree of satisfaction.

Degree of satisfaction? Why not full satisfaction? Well, contentment doesn't breed complacency but it does provide joy on your journey to continue to go to another level.

Even when you are being fruitful, there is always an-other level of fruitfulness that will cause your contentment to be challenged to commit to more! God doesn't produce failures, but people allow failures to be final when He intended them to be stepping-stones to greatness.

I thank God for 2009. It helped me discover 3 life lessons:

- It helped me to refocus on the Word of God and redefine success (Joshua 1:8).

- It helped me learn that my plans without God are worthless. Although I had great intentions and planning, the events of that year helped me understand that my plans won't work if they don't start with God's purpose and then my pursuit of that purpose (Acts 20:24).

- Although those events in my life were painful, it helped me realize there was power in my pain. What power was that? Well, I actually prayed more than I had ever prayed. I sought guidance from the Word more than I ever had, and I looked at my problems differently (Psalm 73).

My pain helped me to see where I was hurting. It positioned me to seek the right help for my hurt and then it redirected me to heal (Psalm 73:14-28).

All of those things caused me to be empowered in such a way that I started to understand there was a power in my pain. My pain helped me to see where I was hurting. It positioned me to seek the right help for my hurt and then it redirected me to heal (Psalm 73:14-28).

Now that I have lived to tell about my pain, it has provided a power in my testimony for those who have gone through something similar, or are currently going through it, or will go through it in the future. Revelation says there is power in our testimony. In other words, there is power in our pain!

Pain can either paralyze you or propel you. Who would sit on a pin that caused pain and stay seated? It should cause you to get up and move! Let your pain propel you into God's plan for your life.

Originally, I thought success had more to do with your possessions, position and power. However, I quickly learned the true definition had more to do with your obedience to God's plan. I also learned that my plans are futile unless they are derived from God's purpose and plan for me.

It also taught me that there is power in my pain. Pain can either paralyze you or propel you. Who would sit on a pin that caused pain and stay seated? It should cause you to get up and move! Let your pain propel you into God's plan for your life.

Your pain could also be an indicator of your ministry, your call, or your area of interest that sensitizes you to the pain of others. When you see that God's plan is best, you interpret every painful situation as an opportunity for spiritual growth.

Redefine Your Success

_____

_____

_____

_____

_____

_____

Once you properly redefine success, your former definition becomes less of the goal and pursuing God's purpose for your life becomes the focus.

But then the question becomes, "How do I get on the road to my ultimate destiny?" The answer is wrapped up in understanding the keys to suCCCCCess. But before we explore the keys, we must first understand the significance of a key.

CHAPTER TWO

The Significance Of A Key

*And I will give you the keys of the Kingdom of Heaven. Whatever you forbid on earth will be forbidden in heaven, and whatever you permit on earth will be permitted in heaven. — **Matthew 16:19***

A key is defined as an instrument that is used to operate a lock. It is also a symbol of authority. There are two parts to a key—the blade, the part that goes into a keyhole; and the bow, the protruding part that allows you to turn the key (see figure 1). The blade is a unique part of the key that allows one to operate a specific lock, unless it's a master key, which operates several locks.

Keys provide an inexpensive method to access the object that it is connected to or protecting its value.

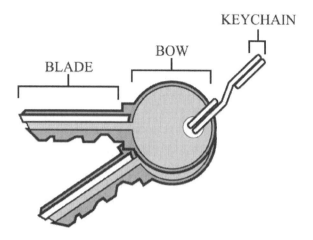

Figure 1

Keys provide an *inexpensive* method to access the object that it is connected to or protecting its value. Keys are essential in our daily lives. It is common for people to carry the set of keys they need for their daily activities around with them, often linked by a key ring.

We rarely think about the true significance of keys in our everyday life. But if I were to take away all keys from you, whether it be your car keys, house keys, garage door codes, computer passwords, phone code, safe or safety deposit box key, you would quickly discover just how significant keys are.

What makes the key so significant is that the keeper of the keys has the power to open and shut the entry to a room, a safe, a vehicle or even information. The keeper of the key has the ability to gain access or restrict access.

What magnifies that significance is the value of what is being opened or accessed; or what is being shut out or denied entry to. In our technologically advanced world, keys can be synonymous with 'keyless' entry access codes, card readers, bar codes, or even Q codes. Needless to say, they have the ability to lock up or lock out, open up or gain access to.

We rarely think about the true significance of keys in our everyday life. But if I were to take away all keys from you, whether it be your car keys, house keys, garage door codes, computer passwords, safe or safety deposit box key, you would quickly discover just how significant keys are.

He trains us, makes sure we take precautions, and that we know his plan and our directional plan.

If that were to happen, you wouldn't be able to lock your house. Risky? You couldn't drive to work. Restricting? Even if you were able to get someone else to give you a ride, you would get to work and wouldn't be able to gain access to your computer or your files in the desk drawer. Unproductive? You then would need to go to the bank to handle some business and you couldn't because you wouldn't have access to your accounts. Costly?

I could go on and on, but I'm sure you get the picture. Without your keys, life could be risky, restricting, unproductive, and costly. Bottom line: Keys are very important!

There are parts of our lives that are extremely valuable, and God has given us the keys to access those precious valuables. God has also given us keys to lock up certain negative elements that would harm our lives. But sadly, many of us have not understood the significance of either of these keys. We haven't fully grasped our ability to access what God has promised and we've also failed to lock up that with which he doesn't want to dirty our lives.

Without your keys, life could be risky, restricting, unproductive, and costly. Bottom line: Keys are very important!

If we understand the key, and what we have access to, or what we have the ability to restrict, and then are given clear direction in how to unlock it and utilize it, or lock it and walk away from it, then we will find out that we are closer to living successfully than we think.

One of the most memorable moments of my life was the moment that I was handed the keys to my very first car at the tender age of 16. It was as though there was a birth of freedom and an instant increase in trust that was placed in me.

For a teenager, this meant my parents trusted me, and I would get the attention I so desired from the girls. It's as though I had suddenly come of age and was ready to take on all that life had to offer for a young, car-driving teenager with so much zeal.

Now, when my son turned 16 years old, I found myself on the other side of this scenario. That's when I realized that my parents most likely did not feel that same sense of joy that I had felt that day.

> *A key is a wonderful thing, but placed in the hands of the wrong person, or used in the wrong manner, can become a dangerous thing. Like most things in life, a key is simply a tool to be either used or abused.*

From my own experience, I have learned that they likely had more of a sense of dread and apprehension at what may lie ahead. And that's when I had my epiphany. Keys give people power. Their maturity, readiness and ability to handle their power is as important for the young driver as it is for the one who gave them the key.

As a parent, I made sure my son got the proper training, took the right safety precautions, and I knew where he was going any time he took the keys and started on his journey. It is no different than how God looks at us. He trains us, makes sure we take precautions, and that we know His plan and our directional plan.

A key is a wonderful thing, but placed in the hands of the wrong person, or used in the wrong manner, can become a dangerous thing. Like most things in life, a key is simply a tool to be either used or abused. It isn't the key that is the problem. It is the man or woman who has the key that determines its use. A key to the bank vault in the hands of a teller is necessary to gain access to the wealth of the depositors when they need to deposit or withdraw. But that key to the bank vault in the hands of a thief becomes a very dangerous thing indeed. In an instant, the thief can bring financial disaster to the bank and all of its depositors. Thank God for depositor's insurance, but no matter how you look at it, that key causes a lot of damage to someone.

Even if you have the Word of God connected to the Power of the Holy Spirit, the key is still useless unless you put it to use.

I want to relate the key described above to this spiritual truth to give you a clearer picture of how the keys of your daily lives are more tied to your life than you think. Think of the blade as the Word of God. Think of the bow as the Holy Spirit (see figure 2).

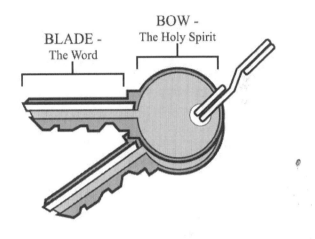

Figure 2

But even if you have the Word of God connected to the power of the Holy Spirit, the key is still useless unless you put it to use. In other words, how would the blade get to the lock? How would the bow be turned, even if the key somehow miraculously got put into the lock?

Here is the bottom line: It is imperative for us to be an active part. We have to provide the actions by inserting the blade into the lock and exercising our faith to turn the bow.

It is our faith working with the Holy Spirit that gives us the torque needed to turn the key. But it will not turn unless we turn it by faith. After all, faith without works (our effort) is dead (see figure 3).

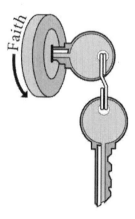

Figure 3

In our lives, we have many keys. That's why we need to connect them with a keychain. As humans, we have a propensity to lose things, which is why a keychain helps us be organized and efficient. While the keychain can seem to be insignificant, it can prove to save a lot of time, energy and effort.

So now that you know the significance of a key, lets learn how to turn it! We will later know which keys to turn in our lives to make sure we enjoy the journey of success.

CHAPTER THREE

You Can't Force Succccccess, But You Can F.A.I.T.H. It!

Uzziah was sixteen years old when he became king, and he reigned in Jerusalem fifty-two years. His mother was Jecoliah from Jerusalem. He did what was pleasing in the LORD's sight, just as his father, Amaziah, had done. Uzziah sought God during the days of Zechariah, who taught him to fear God. And as long as the king sought guidance from the LORD, God gave him success. — **2 Chronicles 26:3-5 NLT**

If the blade and bow of a key is important, it is just as important to learn how to turn the key. The way you do that as we learned earlier is with FAITH. This cannot be illustrated any better than the story of Uzziah. God gave him success! Let's take a look at how and why success was given.

When we look at King Uzziah's story, we find that his success was not by force. Therefore, Uzziah had no power or could not gain success with merely his own strength; otherwise, it would have said Uzziah forced his success.

Nobody can force God to give them success because, if you could have, you would have already. You can't force success! While most of us are trying our best to force our own success, I want to suggest you have no force without faith!

The reality is that God gave him success. The question is, how do we position ourselves for God to give us success?

We must first see what happened before God gave him success. It is found in verse 5b: "As long as the king sought guidance from the Lord." This is a critical element to fully understand. Seeking the Lord is only done by faith, not by force.

Nobody can force God to give them success because, if you could have, you would have already. You can't force success! While most of us are trying our best to force our own success, I want to suggest you have no force without faith! Uzziah teaches us that although you cannot force success, you can faith it!

Follow God's Lead

Uzziah means, "My Strength is Jehovah." His mother's name Jecoliah (Je-co-li-a) means "Jehovah is able." His father's name Amaziah (Am-a-zi-a) means "Jehovah is mighty." Here is a young man who came from a firm foundation. The Lord was all through his lineage. The good news is that regardless of who we are, we all come from a firm foundation. We have all been created by the Almighty God!

So, as we explore King Uzziah's life, we see that his age didn't limit him nor did his family limit him. While some of us may be facing circumstances that are not as ideal as his were, the good news is that God's ability to give us success is not restricted or stifled by our circumstances. There is no worthy success given without the help of our strong, able, almighty God. Our personal efforts are worthless if done outside the will of God.

An additional lesson we learn from Uzziah is that he had great influences. He was influenced by what he saw in his father and what he was taught by Zechariah. While outside influences are important, there is still no substitute for us following God's lead.

Although Uzziah was a young king, please understand your success is not dependent upon your age, nor is it dependent upon your social economic status, your gender, your race, your family origin, your educational level or your financial status.

> *Many of us limit God's plan for our own lives by limiting ourselves by our perceptions of ourselves. Please remember this: So a man thinketh, so is he. In other words, you are what you think of yourself. Your current position or condition is not an indicator of whether or not you can be successful.*

This is liberating to know because many of us limit God's plan for our own lives by limiting ourselves by our perceptions of ourselves. Remember this: So a man thinketh, so is he. In other words, you are what you think of yourself. Your current position or condition is not an indicator of whether or not you can be successful.

> *I know you've heard that success is earned, but I want to suggest that it is given by God. Promotions don't come from the east or the west but from God!*

King Uzziah was taught to lean on God. He relied on God, he sought God, and as long as he placed his faith in God, he was given success. I know you've heard that success is earned, but I want to suggest that it is given by

God. Promotions don't come from the east or the west but from God! Uzziah reigned for 52 years. He was not a one- year success wonder, but he had sustainability and consistency.

In 2 Chronicles 26:5, Uzziah sought God. In Hebrews, the Lord said it like this: "Without faith is it impossible to please God; for he that comes to God must believe that he is, and that he is a rewarder of them that diligently seek him." If you want success, it first comes by seeking God! Whatever you do, please Follow God's Lead!

Apply God's Power

As Uzziah was given success by God in verse 5, he began to apply God's Power in two primary areas of his life – his Work and his Worship! Uzziah teaches us that he understands his calling and his position – King. His job was to protect, provide and prepare his people for success. He walked in his call, his anointing and his gifted area. God helped him while he was doing his job! It is much easier to do the job when you know where you are to be and what you are to be doing. In short, know your role!

As he continued to strive as the King, he did NOT forget the importance of God's house. He built towers in Jerusalem and fortified them which spoke to his close adherence to the worship of God. He cared about the worship of God for himself and his people. So much so that he built towers in the city and the country. Worship should take place wherever you go and wherever you are — near or far, a place of plenty or a desert place. The lesson is that you can access the Power of God through the Worship of God and the work he has called you to do. As you access God's power, whatever you do, PLEASE apply it in every area of your life.

Invest in the Kingdom

King Uzziah teaches us that as you follow God's lead and apply God's power, it is time then to invest in the Kingdom. Notice in verses 9-10, he builds the towers which signifies him investing into the kingdom that God had given him. As he fully leveraged his time and resources into what God had given him, it blessed the people! How? Well you'll notice that he had people working in his fields, vineyards and fertile lands. Therefore, he invested in the people! He not only employed them but gave them the ability to make a living. When you begin to invest in yourself and others, it has a multiplication effect. Investing in the Kingdom always blesses others!

Train for Battle

As you begin to Follow God's lead, Apply God's power, and Invest in the Kingdom, you must then Train for Battle. One thing Uzziah teaches us is that on his journey to success, he certainly realized that he would have to fight, go to battle and he could NOT do it alone.

Uzziah understood the importance of a team. In verse 11, it says he had a well-trained army, ready to go out! Whenever you are training for a battle in your life, you must have the same 3 components Uzziah had.

- A strategy that is clear.

- A team that is prepared.

- A plan that can be executed.

The strategy was clear, as found in verse 13, to support the king against his enemies. Of course, that support was there in order to WIN all battles against the enemy nations. In your life, you must have a strategy to win against all odds.

The team Uzziah had was prepared. Notice in verses 11-15, he shows that he had a great team that was well-organized and trained for battle. I love that Uzziah teaches us that if you and the people connected to you are on the same page, great things can be accomplished. Notice some of the terms used in this passage: well-trained, under the direction, supported the king, provided equipment...these terms ought to be prevalent when we are training to succeed. We have to be trained, we have to be under the direction of the right source, we need to support the King, and when we are provided the whole armor, it puts us in position for our best success. Uzziah by the end of verse 15 had his fame spread far and wide because he was GREATLY helped until he became powerful. Notice he had a strategy, a prepared team and a plan that was executed!

Humble Yourself

My mother always told me, "Experience is the best teacher, especially if it is someone else's"! Well, this is one of those times when we want to learn what NOT to do. God gave Uzziah success by verse 5, made him very powerful by verse 8 and as he continued to follow God's lead, apply God's power, invest in the Kingdom and trained his team for battle, we see that by verse 15, he became famous and powerful. All of this was with God!

Then verse 16 — "But after Uzziah became powerful, his pride led to his downfall". Wow! Pride! He thought of himself more highly than he ought. His success went to his head and his heart! After that, he was unfaithful and then found himself out of place. That's what pride will do to you! He sinned because he was unclean in his heart. He was out of place because he was trying to be a priest when he was designed to be a king.

Whenever you operate in pride, it is not enough to be great in your area of calling. Pride will make you want to be great in somebody else's anointing. Uzziah became great in his own eyes. Satan did the same thing. It wasn't enough to *give* praise; his downfall was in wanting to *receive* praise! His pride came before his destruction.

You can't be successful if you are not willing to confront the big issue! The priest confronted him! Humble yourself under the mighty hand of God and He will exalt you in due season.

In Isaiah 6:1-3, it was in the year King Uzziah died that he saw the Lord. The Lord was sitting on a lofty throne, and the train of His robe filled the Temple. Worship (success of Isaiah) didn't happen until the pride died! Whenever you get rid of pride, it opens up the doors to success.

If you want to remain successful, unlike Uzziah, you might want to kill your pride!

Uzziah helps us to realize that you cannot force success, but you can F.A.I.T.H. it!

- (F)ollow God's Lead
- (A)pply God's Power
- (I)nvest in the Kingdom
- (T)rain for Battle
- (H)umble Yourself

CHAPTER FOUR

The Connection Key

Yes, I am the vine; you are the branches. Those who remain in me, and I in them, will produce much fruit. For apart from me you can do nothing. — *John 15:5*

So now we have learned the significance of a key and how important the Word of God and the Holy Spirit are in working the key. We also learned from Uzziah how to turn the key by F.A.I.T.H. Now it is time to discover the 1st of the 5 Keys That Can Change Your Life. When it comes to the journey to any level of success (or fruitfulness) who you are connected to makes a difference.

Those same Connections can have a positive or negative impact on your destiny. The first key to your success is the Connection Key.

Even in the midst of all the perceived success prior to 2009, I really didn't know how important true Connections were until I was challenged! I thought my Connections were good. After all, I had performed well enough to get a promotion or two in Corporate America and had just leveraged my network to do a few real estate deals and buy my family a big new home. How much better could my Connections have been?

> *If you ever want to rebuild, you must first check the original design of what you are trying to build.*

But after it all came crumbling down, I was forced to check my Connections. I knew God; I thought I knew myself and I certainly knew a lot of people. What I actually learned was the house Kyle built was not on a sure foundation, nor was it built with the proper specifications for long- term success.

If you ever want to build or even rebuild, you must first check the original design of what you are trying to build. It all starts with your Connections!

> *In order for a builder to be successful in building a house, he must first create the blueprint to see the final product before it is even produced.*

There are 3 primary Connections that are critical. Matthew 22:37-40 shares this: "Jesus replied, 'You must love the Lord your God with all your heart, all your soul, and all your mind. This is the first and greatest commandment. A second is equally important: 'Love your neighbor as yourself.' The entire law and all the demands of the prophets are based on these two commandments.'"

- Connection with God

- Connection with Yourself

- Connection to Other People

If you want success in the finished product of your life, you must go back to the designer—the builder of your life—God. If you connect to God, it will unlock the first key to putting you on the suCCCCCess journey.

Connection with God

Independent of the first Connection there is no success. Again, I am not talking about the world's definition. In order for a builder to be successful in building a house, he must first create the blueprint to see the final product before it is even produced.

If there are any questions about how the house will be built, you will need to go to the builder who designed it. This is no different in our own lives. If there are any questions on the design of our lives, (like what is supposed to be in it or what's supposed to happen), the only one who knows is the designer: God.

So if you want success in the finished product of your life, you must go back to the designer—the builder of your life—God. When you connect with God, it will keep you on the suCCCCCess journey.

Connecting with God puts you on the path to being able to connect with yourself. How can you love who you do not know? Loving yourself is critical in this process.

Connection with Yourself

Connecting with God puts you on the path to being able to connect with yourself. How can we truly love ourselves, if we really don't know and appreciate who God made us to be? Loving yourself is critical in this process.

How do you connect with yourself? Knowing who you are and who God made you to be helps you realize your significance and your importance.

To follow the example of building the house, once the builder lays out the blueprint, you realize you are the General Contractor of this building. Now that you know the plan (blueprint), you must then recognize your strengths, weaknesses, what resources you have and the project plan to begin to build the house.

This is important to know before you bring others into the building process. What are you good at? What resources do you have? Do you have the proper plan to put this all together based upon what the designer intended? Connect to yourself.

> *Even when God gives you the blueprint for your life, most people get stuck at connecting with themselves. Why? Cause we do not want to take an honest inventory of who we are personally, professionally, spiritually, financially, socially or even physically.*

I'm sure you have probably heard the saying, "If you fail to plan, then plan to fail." I'd like to change it up a bit and say it like this, "If you plan to succeed, then you need to succeed at planning."

Even when God gives you the blueprint for your life, most people get stuck at connecting with themselves. Why? Because we do not want to take an honest inventory of who we are personally, professionally, spiritually, financially, socially or even physically.

In order to be the best we can be, we need to do a SWOT analysis on our own lives. What is a SWOT? It is simply assessing your Strengths, Weaknesses, Opportunities and Threats. On the next three pages you'll find out how in the Personal SWOT Template.

Personal SWOT Template

You are fearfully and wonderfully made—so what do you think God put you on earth to do?

Your Purpose:

_____

_____

Strengths

Strength – a quality or state of being strong

Identify 3-5 examples

What do you do well? What do you do better than others? What competencies do you possess to fulfill your purpose? ***Essentially, what are you great at?***

Weaknesses

Weakness – a state or quality of being weak; lack of strength

Identify 3-5 examples

What do you NOT do well? What do others do better than you? What skills of yours need improvement in order to fulfill your purpose? ***Essentially, what do you need to work on?***

Opportunities

Opportunity – A situation favorable for attainment of a goal

Identify 3-5 examples

Do you see a place where you can do what you are called to do? Do you see a need around you? What things can you leverage to help you fulfill your purpose? ***Essentially, what are you best suited for?***

Threats

Threat – An indication or warning of probable trouble

Identify 3-5 examples

What are your personal/internal hindrances? What are your social, financial, professional or other external hindrances? What is/could hold you back from fulfilling your purpose? ***Essentially, what stands in your way of success?***

1 — Write down your purpose
2 — Complete this SWOT analysis
3 — Take action to:

> *a — Strengthen your strengths*
> *b — Overcome your weaknesses*
> *c — Leverage your opportunities*
> *d — Defend against your threats*

The SWOT helped me realize that God wired me, made me, and purposed me to be *me*! And now I embrace it and leverage it!

> *Those who consider themselves successful will never be able to say it was done all on their own. Success is never selfish! It always involves others.*

Connection with Other People

Connecting with other people is also critical in this process. Any life built will not only include God and the person, but it always involves other people!

Those who consider themselves successful will never be able to say it was done all on their own. Success is never selfish! It always involves others.

In the case of building the house, the general contractor of a project will need to engage other people to do significant yet coordinated functions in order to build the house to the specs of the builder.

You will need the electrician to run conduit and wiring, you need the carpenter to build the walls, rooms and finishes, and you need the interior decorator to decorate the home, and many more to make sure you build a house that you're not only able to live in, but enjoy as well.

I can remember going through the latter part of 2009 and realizing that God had put people around me to help me. But I didn't see their purpose in my life until I reconnected with God and understood myself. I then understood how important my network was. The great news is that while in some cases it identified people I needed to connect with, it also identified people I did not need to be connected to. I began thinking about the importance of Connections.

Our branches can only flourish if they are all connected to the true vine. How connected are the branches of your life?

Importance of Your Connection

The importance of Connection is illustrated best in John 15:1-8. This scripture gives us a great way to see the importance of a Connection, what it can produce, and what it requires to have even more fruitfulness. If you are ever going to travel down the road of your suCCCCCess journey, you will need to understand these principles.

John 15:1 says, "I am the true vine (Jesus is the Ultimate Connection) and my Father is the gardener (God makes the Connection)."

The good news about the gardener is, he knows what he is working with and understands the importance of the true vine.

He also recognizes branches that are truly connected to the vine. This is critical to know because it is the gardener who does the work, as long as the branch simply responds to what comes from the vine when the gardener touches it!

Our branches can only flourish if they are all connected to the true vine. How connected are the branches of your life? Your financial/stewardship branch? Your educational branch? Your spiritual branch? Your economic branch? Your physical branch? Your physiological branch? Your fitness branch? Your health branch? Your overall branch?

Staying in the Word will keep you clean and connected.

John 15:2 says, "He cuts off every branch in me that bears no fruit."

God cuts off Connections with no fruit, while every branch that does bear fruit he prunes so that it will become even more fruitful. He cleans up Connections through cutting. So the question is what area or unfruitful branch in your life needs to be cut away? Anything that keeps you from being fruitful , you need to consider cutting out of your life? For some, it may be an unhealthy habit. Whatever it is, it is worth it?

John 15:3 says, "You are already clean because of the word I have spoken to you." Staying in the Word will keep you clean and connected.

John 15:4 says, "Remain in me, and I will remain in you. No branch can bear fruit by itself; it must remain in the vine." You cannot do it alone. You must be connected. If you want to be fruitful your Connection must have consistency. Your fruitfulness is never by yourself. Stay connected and you can bear fruit!

John 15:5 says, "I am the vine; you are the branches. If a man remains in me and I in him, he will bear much fruit; apart from me you can do nothing." You may appear to grow, but without consistent Connection it will not be useful. Remaining connected will help you go from bear fruit to bearing MUCH fruit! More than you did before you were consistent!

John 15:6 says, "If anyone does not remain in me, he is like a branch that is thrown away and withers; such branches are picked up, thrown into the fire and burned." If you don't get connected, whatever you produce won't last. You don't want all that you have done to be 'thrown' away or 'burnt' up!

John 15:7 says, "If you remain in me and my words remain in you, ask whatever you wish, and it will be given you." Your Connection allows your wishes to be granted. Do you want to be given whatever you wish for? Yes? Well, remain connected to God and have his Word remain in you!

John 15:8 says, "This is to my Father's glory, that you bear much fruit, showing yourselves to be my disciples." Your Connection will produce fruitfulness in your life and those of others. Disciples always produce and they always multiply.

Show me someone who is successful and I'll show you someone who reproduces his success in other people. The biblical example is Jesus! He mentored 3, discipled 12, but impacted the masses!

Show me someone who is successful and I'll show you someone who reproduces his success in other people. The biblical example is Jesus! He mentored 3, discipled 12, but impacted the masses!

Since 2009, I have been able to impact more lives from what I thought was my downfall. As long as I am connected, I am on my way to fully enjoying my journey no matter how many twists and turns, peaks or valleys, deserts or rivers I encounter. My Connections truly made a difference and they will continue to do so!

Once you utilize your Connection Key, it is time to learn about your Calling Key.

CHAPTER FIVE

The Calling Key

Therefore I, a prisoner for serving the Lord, beg you to lead a life worthy of your calling, for you have been called by God. — **Ephesians 4:1**

Do you know what your calling is? If so, what is it?

_____

_____

_____

_____

If you don't know it, are you ready to discover it? Regardless of whether you know it or not, here are some truths that you should understand, embrace and walk in.

A calling is for anyone who has a purpose; this means EVERYONE has a calling!

There are 3 truths about your life and the Calling Key:

- You are undeniably called by God to create change in the lives of the people you are connected to.

- You are spiritually and naturally gifted to meet a need.

- You are a sum total of your life's experiences, and if you find your calling it will all be used to better your life and the lives of others.

In order to discover your calling, you must understand what a "Calling" is. It is a strong inner impulse toward a particular course of action. The course of action for your life is your calling on your life! What is your God-given purpose for being on earth? Callings are not exclusive to those who are pastors, church leaders or ministers. A calling is for anyone who has a purpose; this means EVERYONE has a calling.

In his book *Purpose Driven Life*, Rick Warren asks the question, "What on earth are you here for?" He also says: "It's not about you." If it is not about you, then who is it about? When you find out the answer to that question, you will find out why you are on earth!

Your calling has been already determined so it is never the case that you don't have a calling; it's a question of whether you have found out what it is!

The Passion Indicator

So how do you start living out your calling? First, you must recognize your calling can be found through your passion. In other words, your passion can serve as an indicator of your calling:

- What drives you? What are you passionate about?

- What do you have a heart for?

- What motivates you to reach out to and care for people?

- What situation drives you to act on behalf of change?

Action

If money was no issue or you didn't have a 9-5 job, what would you do with your time based upon your passion?

The People Indicator

Once you recognize your passion, ask yourself who do you feel called to help, serve or work with the most?

- Who do you gravitate towards?

- Who do you influence?

- Who do you socialize with and relate to?

Action

In regard to the people you relate to the most, in a healthy and productive way, what do those relationships tell you about your calling?

The Place Indicator

Once you identify your passion and the people, ask yourself where do I walk out and work out my call? Where have I been placed to make all of this work?

- What environment am I most comfortable with?

- What place do I seem to flourish?

- Where do I always seem to end up when I pursue my passion?

- Where would I need to be if I went to serve the people I have compassion for?

Action

What place, area or location will allow me to carry out my calling?

Jeremiah 1:4-5 says, "The Word of the Lord came to me, saying, 'Before I formed you in the womb I knew you, before you were born I set you apart.'"

> *God has already said that he knew you and set you a part. What is implied there is that you are set apart for a purpose.*

Your calling has been already determined, so it is never the case that you don't have a calling; it's a question of whether you have found out what it is!

God has already said that he knew you and set you apart. What is implied there is that you were set apart for a purpose. Refer back to your SWOT Analysis. In other words, you were born for a reason and you are called to do something while you are here. We are people of calling and destiny. You are undeniably *called* by God to create change in the lives of the people you are *connected* to.

> *Your success is tied to your calling and your Connections. You will never be able to be successful without it impacting others!*

1 Peter 2:9 says, "For you are a chosen people. You are royal priests, a holy nation, God's very own possession. As a result, you can show others the goodness of

God, for he called you out of the darkness into his wonderful light."

Every situation in your life and your path or plight is
all for a reason. Your call will definitely include leveraging that reality to help others! Your success is tied to
your Calling and your Connections. You will never be
able to be successful without it impacting others!

A calling is not about what you do but *who* you are.
When you figure out your calling, at least two certainties
will always show up!

Conviction

I ran across a quote by David A. Bednar that summa-
rizes the importance of conviction, *"Sometimes we may
ask God for success, and He gives us physical and men-
tal stamina. We might plead for prosperity, and we
receive enlarged perspective and increased patience, or
we petition for growth and are blessed with the gift of
grace. He may bestow upon us conviction and confidence as we strive to achieve worthy goals."* It is the
conviction and confidence that will keep you focused on
your calling when everything may not go your way or
when things are not happening as fast as you like.

As you start to walk out your calling, your conviction
for completing your purpose kicks in and you will find
yourself more determined, more focused and more ener-
gized than you have ever been. You will find yourself
looking at what has happened to you in the past as opportunities to propel you within your purpose!

This is best summarized by a quote by Dr. Martin Luther King, Jr., *"My personal trials have also taught me the value of unmerited suffering. As my sufferings mounted I soon realized that there were two ways that I could respond to my situation: either to react with bitterness or seek to transform the suffering into a creative force. I decided to follow the latter course. Recognizing the necessity for suffering I have tried to make of it virtue. If only to save myself from bitterness, I have attempted to see my personal ordeals as an opportunity to transform myself and heal the people involved in the tragic situation, which now obtains. I have lived these last few years with the conviction that unearned suffering is redemptive."* Simply said, Conviction is a by-product of leveraging your Calling Key.

Compassion

Compassion is defined as a feeling of deep sympathy and sorrow for another who is stricken by misfortune, accompanied by a strong desire to alleviate the suffering. When you unlock the Calling Key not only does your conviction show up, but also your compassion. We can relate to that. Many of us are motivated to love and serve out of recognition of someone else's need. We are moved to action when we realize that we can meet a need, especially when we are walking out our calling or fulfilling our purpose in life.

Sometimes we refer to this as "having a passion" or "having a heart" for a specific type of people or specific situation. God often places us in the people group that we are most equipped to reach. Whatever people group God calls you to love and serve, it will be made up of those who you are to impact. Remember, success is never just about you, it always includes someone else.

When we live our Calling in our own strength, the results can be less than what we hoped for, but when we live our calling with the proper Connections, it can yield the fruitfulness that not only blesses us but blesses many others.

Many people recognize their calling, but don't recognize God. Your call only comes after your ultimate Connection. When we live our Calling in our own strength, the results can be less than what we hoped for, but when we live our calling with the proper Connections, it can yield the fruitfulness that not only blesses us but blesses many others.

A calling lived through God's power and direction is life changing. It sets people free from their oppression and rescues people. It speaks truth into their lives and points lost people back to their calling. Our calling is completed through our Connection with Jesus Christ.

2 Thessalonians 1:11-12 says, "So we keep on praying for you, asking our God to enable you to live a life

worthy of his call. May he give you the power to accomplish all the good things your faith prompts you to do. Then the name of our Lord Jesus will be honored because of the way you live, and you will be honored along with him. This is all made possible because of the grace of our God and Lord, Jesus Christ."

> *Your simple act of love can be the difference-maker in someone else's life. Make a difference in the lives of the people you connect with.*

Using your Connections can help you understand or solidify your calling! As you go throughout your week, ask yourself: "What is their situation?" and "What can I do to help change that situation?" Your simple act of love can be the difference-maker in someone else's life. Make a difference in the lives of the people you connect with - at home with your family, at work with your coworkers, with your friends or at school with your classmates. Wherever you are, MAKE A DIFFERENCE by operating in your calling!

Remember, God wants your life to show others His goodness and he wants your life to shine His light into others' darkness. The question is, "Do you believe that God can use you to change someone's life?"

Your Calling will Produce P.O.W.E.R.

(P)assion – your passion is a key indicator of your calling.

(O)pportunities – when you begin to walk in your calling, you will be able to readily identify opportunities to put your calling to use. Have they always been there? Possibly. But because you are connected and have accepted your calling, they will become more apparent!

(W)illingness – once the opportunities are identified, you have to be willing to accept, embrace and meet the needs of those opportunities.

(E)mpowerment – this willingness will surely unlock a level of empowerment to not only get the job done but to excel in every opportunity.

(R)esults – The results will be inevitable because you have unleashed and unlocked the door to fruitfulness. The fact that you are connected to God and obedient to your calling will surely produce fruit/results every time!

Once you utilize your Connection and Calling Keys (having tapped into the P.O.W.E.R.), you are now ready to unleash the many possibilities and opportunities by using your Creative Key.

CHAPTER SIX

The Creative Key

Don't compare yourself with others. Each of you must take responsibility for doing the creative best you can with your own life. — Galatians 6:5 (Msg)

The Scriptures have proven that God can create solutions when there are none. The Bible begins with the creation of the "heavens and the earth" and ends with the creation of the new heavens and new earth which are to come.

God is a creative being; we are made in His image; therefore, we are inherently creative. This is not a matter of being "gifted." There is no gift of creativity. It is a matter of expressing the creativity that we all inherently possess.

We value creativity because we are inherently creative. "So God created man in his own image, in the image of God he created him; male and female he created them" (Genesis 1:27, NIV).

God is a creative being; we are made in His image; therefore, we are inherently creative. This is not a matter of being "gifted." There is no gift of creativity. It is a matter of expressing the creativity that we all inherently possess.

It is amazing that when you start doing what you are called to do, how many new ideas flow through your mind. The question is what do you do with those ideas, thoughts, dreams, visions?

It is amazing that when you start doing what you are called to do, how many new ideas flow through your mind. The question is what do you do with those ideas, thoughts, dreams, visions?

Many of us let them lie dormant or even allow self-hatred or doubt to throw the thought away. From this day forward, when an idea comes into your mind that is related to your Connection and your Call, do these 3 things:

1. Write it down!
2. Believe it to be possible!
3. Do something about it!

After being more conscious about my Connection and once I began to truly walk in my Calling, I was amazed how many ideas started to flow through my mind. I was reminded of past ideas that I shook off as impossible, only to realize that they could have catapulted me into my destiny.

Decide that today you will begin to do something about those ideas. Don't let your past, your fear, or anything or anyone stop you from unlocking the doors of your creativity.

Here is what you do not want to do. Do not wallow in the indecisive paralysis of yesterday. This is the time to "chalk up" all of the past missed creative opportunities as a learning experience; then dust off some of those ideas if they are still relevant today and position yourself to do something about all the creative ideas from this day forward. Decide that today you will begin to do something about those ideas. Don't let your past, your fear, or anything or anyone stop you from unlocking the doors of your creativity.

Although this chapter may be short, it is one of the most important ones. Your creativity could unleash success quicker than you ever thought, take you further than you ever intended to go, and cause you to leave a legacy you didn't think was possible. This is all possible because you have taken responsibility for doing your creative best with your own life, as Galatians says.

Here are actions that you can take to stimulate an environment that fosters your creativity!

Ways to Stimulate a Creative Environment

Unlock your Imagination
- Think and dream often.
- If you had no limits, what would you do?
- Visit new places to spark your creativity.

Going with the Flow
- Don't concern yourself with what others think.

Direct your Focus
- Visualize a new reality. What does it look like?
- Focus more on what could be versus what was or wasn't!
- Brainstorm frequently.

Limit Distractions
- Get some rest. Relax. It will help. When you are tired, you get easily distracted.

- Protect your quiet time.
- Focus on your To-Do List. That helps you fulfill your purpose.

Knowing Your "Time" to Be Creative
- If you are a morning person, get up early. Read the Word, meditate, journal your thoughts, ideas, dreams, aspirations and visions!
- If you are a night owl, do it before you go to bed!
- If you think well while exercising, get SoundCloud on your phone and record your thoughts while you are on the treadmill.

Know What Stimulates You
- If listening to music sparks something in you, have a pen and notebook ready as you listen.

So as long as your faith is in God, you are in good hands. Ask Peter! He did something that had not been done by anyone other than God. He creatively walked on water!

You must have the determination to create the environment that will allow your creativity to flourish. When your creativity grows, please make sure you remain open to risk taking. After all, faith requires risk.

So as long as your faith is in God, you are in good hands. Ask Peter! He did something that had not been done by anyone other than God. He creatively walked on water! He took a risk; he was focused; and he knew his time. It wasn't until he lost his focus and took his eye off of the goal that he began to sink.

Here are some things and situations that stifle creativity. Also, here are actions that you can take to overcome the hindrance and allow your creativity to flourish!

Overcoming Hindrances of Creativity

Fear of Failure
- Learn from your past failure and trust in God's plan!

Fear of Ambiguity
- Trust in God who will help you overcome what you don't know!

Lack of Confidence
- Prepare and plan as if it all depends on you, but execute and trust as if it all depends on God.

Nay Sayers - Other People
- Believe what God says about you, not others!

Too much Analysis
- Pray, listen, hear, and act on what God says!

False Limits
- Although you may have limits, the one you believe in doesn't! Believe in Him!

The fact that you are reading this book right now is a testament of this Creative Key. I have had this 'crazy' idea of writing books for several years; however, because I am an Industrial Engineer and MBA by education and spent most of my career in Sales, IT, Operations Management using my gifts and talents to talk, analyze , and manage, I thought I was FAR from 'writing' a book. After all, I AM NOT A WRITER! ☺ But I decided to not let fear, my limitations or my creative thoughts keep me from doing the "impossible" — for me to WRITE a book.

I've made up my mind to do what Myles Munroe said, "Don't die old, die empty." Since I have several books in me, I would rather get them out of me than to allow my own self- inflicted limitations to have me die old and full of ideas. For me, I am unlocking my Creative Key and committing myself to dying empty!

Once you utilize your Connection, Calling, and Creative Keys, it is time for the very important Communication Key.

CHAPTER SEVEN

The Communication Key

"And the Lord answered me, and said, 'Write the vision, and make it plain upon tables, that he may run that readeth it.'" — **Habakkuk 2:2**

Once you start to experience the creativity that only comes when you have tapped into all the ideas, dreams and visions that arise from your purpose and plan, it is time to use the communication key. This key will help you creatively translate your Calling into a documented plan of action.

> *It is true, as deemed by Habakkuk 2:2, if you want people to help you run with your vision, than you have to be able to read it and it must be plain.*

I was once told if it is not written it is not real. I believe it because I can talk all day long about a business plan and having the right elevator pitch, but the bank will want a documented business plan that will give details of what I'm talking about.

Communication is key to your success. Why? Because if you fail to plan, then plan to fail. A plan helps you stay on course; it helps you clearly define what success looks like and gives you the plan of action to get it done!

It is true, as deemed by Habakkuk 2:2, if you want people to help you run with your vision, than you have to be able to read it and it must be plain.

What better time to write your vision down than right now? This will help bring clarity to your plan. This will help solidify in your own heart and mind that you have something to go after.

When you get connected with others who are brought into your path to assist and challenge you, it will be clear what role they play.

Communication is key to your success. Why? Because if you fail to plan, then plan to fail. A plan helps you stay on course; it helps you clearly define what success looks like and gives you the plan of action to get it done!

Strategic Planning 101

Vision: What do you want to be or where do you want to go?

Mission: What you do, why and for whom.

Guiding Principles: How you plan to accomplish the MISSION and VISION.

Action Plans: The specific aligned actions used to accomplish the MISSION and VISION. The actions must be S.M.A.R.T. (Specific Measurable Attainable Realistic with a Timeframe) objectives.

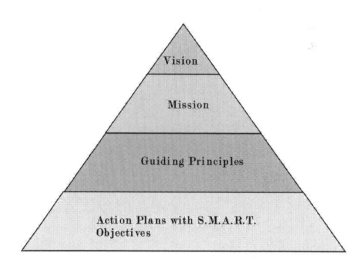

Benefits of strategic planning:

- Provide clearer focus.

- Produce more efficiency and effectiveness.

- Ensure the proper alignment of action plans for the vision/mission.

In short, it is a process to ensure action plans support your ultimate mission and vision.

Strategic Planning Problem...

No Implemented Plan!

The reason most of us do NOT create a strategic plan is because action planning may seem too detailed and take too much time. Therefore, action planning is too often ignored, leaving the results of earlier stages of our planning as "Pie in the Sky" — useless philosophical statements with no grounding in the day-to-day realities of our lives - making the meaningful suCCCCCess Keys utterly useless.

As Habakkuk suggests, you cannot run with something you haven't read and you cannot read something that hasn't been written, and you cannot write something that hasn't been given by a Vision, and you cannot have a vision without being Connected with a Calling! So you see how important this Communication Key is!?!

Once you develop your strategic plan, it requires you to align and execute against your action plans to reach your goals. In addition, you must evaluate and hold yourself accountable to the action plans and refine/revise as necessary to stay on task.

What if the Action Plans are Misaligned?

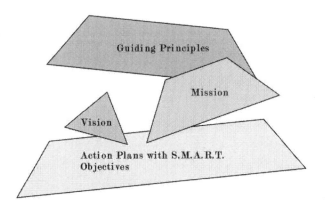

When key elements are misaligned, the pyramid is NOT as designed, thereby limiting its beauty and its appeal. This is also true of our lives and our goals when they are misaligned.

Often times, when our actions plans are misaligned, it causes us to take longer than we intended, cause more frustration than we wanted and puts us in the position not to reach our goal. The simple way to ensure that your action plans are aligned with your goal is to ask yourself one simple question – Is this action going to help me get closer to my goal?

My Strategic Plan for Success
(See Back of Book for Worksheets)

Date:_____

Vision: What do you want to be or where do you want to go:

_____
_____
_____
_____
_____
_____

Mission: What you do, why and for whom.

_____
_____
_____
_____
_____
_____

Guiding Principles: How you plan to accomplish the MISSION and VISION.

_____
_____
_____
_____

_____

_____

Action Plans: The specific aligned actions used to accomplish the MISSION and VISION.

_____

_____

_____

_____

_____

_____

Purpose

To create an action plan for accomplishing your mission to get to your vision.

Directions

1. Using this form as a template, develop an action plan for each goal identified. *Modify the form as needed to fit your unique context.*

2. Distribute copies of each action plan to those that you will collaborate with to accomplish your goal.

3. Keep copies handy to bring to review and update regularly.

Ideas — Dreams — Aspirations — Vision
What Do You See? Write it Down:

_____

_____

_____

_____

_____

_____

_____

_____

_____

_____

_____

Goal

Action Steps: What Will Be Done?

Responsibilities: Who Will Do It?

Timeline: By When (Day/Month)?

Resources: A) Resources Available; B) Resources Needed (financial, human, political, other):

Potential Barriers: A) What Individuals or organization might resist? B) How?

Communication Plan: Who Is Involved? What Methods? How often?

Once you utilize your Connection Key, your Calling Key, your Creativity Key and your Communication Key, you must then stay on course by using your Commitment Key!

CHAPTER EIGHT

The Commitment Key

"Commit your actions to the Lord, and your plans will succeed."
— **Proverbs 16:3**

In the Old Testament, we find the prophet Elijah and the calling of his attendant and eventual successor. 1 Kings 19:15-21 says, "The Lord said to Elijah, 'Go back the way you came, and go to the Desert of Damascus. When you get there, anoint . . . Elisha son of Shaphat from Abel Meholah to succeed you as prophet' … So Elijah went from there and found Elisha son of Shaphat. He was plowing with twelve yoke of oxen, and he himself was driving the twelfth pair. Elijah went up to him and threw his cloak around him.

Elisha then left his oxen and ran after Elijah. 'Let me kiss my father and mother goodbye,' he said, 'and then I will come with you.' 'Go back,' Elijah replied. 'What have I done to you?' So Elisha left him and went back. He took his yoke of oxen and slaughtered them. He burned the plowing equipment to cook the meat and gave it to the people, and they ate. Then he set out to follow Elijah and became his attendant."

What does it mean to be committed? It means making a firm choice. It means not worrying about keeping your options open, or leaving yourself a way out.

Here we see Elisha, a simple farmer, who is suddenly and unexpectedly approached by the famous prophet Elijah and invited to accompany him and serve him as his personal attendant.

When Elisha requests time to first go home and say goodbye to his parents, Elijah makes it clear that the decision to come is entirely Elisha's to make. "What have I done to you?" means, in essence, "What claim do I have on you?" And the implied answer is "none."

In other words, Elisha is free to stay or go. In response, Elisha not only chooses to accept the call, but he slaughters his oxen and feeds them to his neighbors, burning his plowing equipment to cook the meat. By doing this, he publicly and irrevocably declares his intention to leave his former way of life and follow Elijah.

My topic is commitment, and this story gives an illustration of that concept—burning the plows. Pressing towards your goal at all cost is the principle.

You've heard of "burning your bridges." Now you've heard of "burning your plows." But what does it mean to be committed? It means making a firm choice. It means not worrying about keeping your options open, or leaving yourself a way out.

God isn't calling us to be reckless or foolhardy. He doesn't want us to just rush into things without counting the cost. But once we've determined the path we're going to take; once we've discerned to the best of our ability what God is calling us to do, then what He wants are sold-out followers who won't look back when the going gets tough.

It means pursuing something wholeheartedly, with no contingency plans to fall back on. It means being 100% sold out to a person or a cause or a goal, not holding anything back, not keeping anything in reserve. The problem with many of us is that we fall victim to the enemies of commitment – Caution, Risk, and What ifs.

Now, the idea of being this committed—to anyone or anything—makes some people uncomfortable. What if the person, project or plan you've committed yourself to lets you down? What if the cause or results turn out to be not as worthy as you thought? There's a lot to be said for caution. God isn't calling us to be reckless or foolhardy.

> *What He wants are disciples who are so committed to Him that they will burn their bridges, or their boats, or their oxen-- disciples who will discard whatever is holding them back and follow Him wherever He leads.*

He doesn't want us to just rush into things without counting the cost. But once we've determined the path we're going to take, once we've discerned to the best of our ability our God- given purpose or plan, then it is time to get going, even if the going gets tough! As Proverbs says, "Commit your actions to the Lord, and your plans will succeed."

As you start or continue on your journey of suCCCCCess, I want you to ponder these questions:

- Will you be motivated by your faith or paralyzed by your fear?
- Will you be driven by your belief or burdened by your doubt?
- Will you have the can do attitude or will you always think you can't do?
- Will you or might you?

On April 21st, in the year 1519, the Spanish explorer Hernando Cortez sailed into the harbor of Vera Cruz, Mexico. He brought with him about 600 men and over the next two years his vastly outnumbered forces were able to defeat Montezuma and all the warriors of the Aztec empire, making Cortez the conqueror of all Mexico. How was this incredible feat accomplished, when two prior expeditions failed even to establish a colony on Mexican soil?

Here's the secret. Cortez knew from the very beginning that he and his men faced incredible odds. He knew that the road before them would be dangerous and difficult. He knew that his men would be tempted to abandon their quest and return to Spain.

And so, as soon as Cortez and his men had come ashore and unloaded their provisions, he ordered their entire fleet of eleven ships destroyed. His men stood on the shore and watched as their only possibility of retreat burned and sank.

And from that point on, they knew there was no turning back. Nothing lay behind them but empty ocean. Their only option was to go forward, to conquer or die.

You've heard of "burning your bridges" and "burning your plows" and now you've heard of "burning your boats." Some of us have allowed bridges or plows/bulls or even boats to keep us from committing to pursuing our suCCCCCess journey. But we need to learn that commitment is when there is no other option to turn back!

What do you do when the feeling leaves as you begin your journey? The answer is to stay committed!

"Commitment means staying loyal to what you said you were going to do, long after the mood you said it in has left you" — **Unknown Author**

The SuCCCCCess Journey for me has become a way of life. I choose to use these 5 Keys That Can, That Have and Will Continue to Change My Life!

Will you use these 5 Keys That Can Change Your Life?

- Connection Key
- Calling Key
- Creative Key
- Communication Key
- Commitment Key

CHAPTER NINE

Finding Joy During the Journey

"Then they said, 'Ask God whether or not our journey will be successful.' 'Go in peace,' the priest replied. 'For the Lord is watching over your journey.'" — Judges 18:5-6

It doesn't matter where you are right now or what road you find yourself on — because you are in the right spot to begin your journey to success.

A journey is defined as an act of traveling from one place to another. You are now on a new road to your success and it is time to find the joy during this journey.

Go in peace, for the Lord is watching over your journey. It doesn't get any better than that!

We often feel like Judges 18:5-6, which says: "Then they said, 'Ask God whether or not our journey will be successful.' 'Go in peace,' the priest replied. 'For the Lord is watching over your journey.'"

Knowing the Lord is watching over your journey ought to give you confidence in knowing it will be all right. Since that is the reality, we might as well find joy because of the exact thing the priest said. Go in peace, for the Lord is watching over your journey. It doesn't get any better than that!

It is my hope that you have been educated, equipped and feel empowered now with what it is that you are called to do.

Nike has made the phrase "Just Do It" famous; however, we should make it our battle cry! After learning what success is, the significance of a key, the keys to suCCCCCess, and knowing we cannot force success but we can F.A.I.T.H. it, it is now time to embrace the joy of the journey.

I've learned that I can deal with uncertainties and unknowns in life, as long as I am educated, equipped, and empowered with a focus or a goal. It is my hope that you have been educated, equipped and feel empowered now to accomplish your goals.

The final part of this process is not approaching this with a degree of trepidation or fear or even anxiety, but finding the joy during this journey. I do not know how long of a journey you have, but what I do know is you might as well find joy while on the road to your success.

Once a man has made a commitment to a way of life, he puts the greatest strength in the world behind him. It's something we call heart power. Once a man has made his commitment, nothing will stop him short of success. **~ Vincent Thomas Lombardi**

Every day you wait is another day that you will never get back again. The most important thing is not to be bitter about life's disappointments but use them to make you better. Becoming better not bitter – it is your choice!

Learn to let go of the past. Don't be afraid to make mistakes, because most of the time the greatest rewards come from doing the things that scare you the most. Maybe you'll get everything you wish for. Maybe you'll get more than you ever could have imagined. Who knows where life can take you? The road is long and in the end the journey is your destination. **~ Author Unknown.**

Welcome to "Your" SuCCCCCess Journey!

I can't wait to hear your success stories. You can tweet me @kylepmarshall, Facebook me at Kyle Marshall, or Instagram me at kylepmarshall or even email me at kylepmarshall@yahoo.com. I want to hear about your suCCCCCess Journey!

About The Author

Kyle Marshall is a graduate of Purdue University with a Bachelor of
Science degree in Industrial Engineering. He earned a Master in
Business Administration from the University of Illinois at Chicago
with an emphasis in Finance and Strategic Management. Kyle has a
wealth of diverse experience in Operations, Program & Project
Management, Information Technology, Customer Service, and Sales
Management. He has worked for several Fortune 250 companies;
such as Sara Lee Corporation, W. W. Grainger and DuPont
Pharmaceuticals in roles ranging from Business System
Management to District Sales Manager to Program

Management. Kyle is honored to have played an instrumental role in helping them all become more efficient and effective through process improvements and business development strategies. He joined Redbox in a Business Improvement role focused on driving strategic improvement activities across the business but now serves as Program Manager for Redbox Customer Service Department.

Kyle Marshall is a passionate teacher and expositor of the Word of God. He has shown himself to be an effective leader, administrator, and teacher while mentoring others in ministry development. He attended Grace Theological Seminary to receive a Masters in Ministry degree with a focus in Urban Ministry and Leadership. Kyle Marshall also serves as an Associate Pastor and Elder for one of the most progressive churches on the South Side of Chicago, New Beginnings Church of Chicago under the leadership of Pastor Corey B. Brooks. Kyle continues to leverage his education, his professional expertise and ministry experiences in helping organizations — both For Profit and Not-for-Profit — become more efficient and effective. The primary areas of training & development are in Leadership, Strategic Planning, Change Management, Team Building and a host of other key developmental workshops.

On a personal note, Kyle is married to the lovely, beautiful and wonderful Tahi S. Marshall. He is also a proud father of three wonderful children: Omar, Kayla, and Anaya. In addition to spending quality time with his wife and children, Kyle dedicates his time in fulfilling his personal mission — To Help Others Help Themselves.

About SermonToBook.Com

SermonToBook.com began with a simple belief: that sermons should be touching lives, *not* collecting dust. That's why we turn sermons into high-quality books that are accessible to people all over the globe.

Turning your sermon or sermon series into a book exposes more people to God's Word, better equips you for counseling, accelerates future sermon prep, adds credibility to your ministry, and even helps make ends meet during tight times.

John 21:25 tells us that the world itself couldn't contain the books that would be written about the work of Jesus Christ. Our mission is to try anyway. Because, in Heaven, there will no longer be a need for sermons or books. Our time is now.

If God so leads you, we'd love to work with you on ır sermon or sermon series.

'isit www.sermontobook.com to learn more.

YOUR *PROBLEMS*
HAVE *PURPOSE*

Understanding God's plan
for your life

Steve Bozeman

All Problems in your past, present and future have a Purpose to fulfill in your life! The problems you are dealing with are leaving you frustrated, depressed and feeling like God has abandoned you. You've been praying for relief and you've even tried to borrow relief, but nothing is working. You constantly question, "Why all of these problems, God?"

Your Problems Have Purpose is an engaging book, full of practical life-application principles including:

- Discovering who you are in Christ
- Growing in God's purpose for you
- Learning how to overcome the fact that brokenness hurts
- Submitting to God's will for your life and living successfully

Additionally you'll learn…

- Exactly how God uses your problems to develop your purpose
- Why God uses problems to protect you from yourself
- What your purpose cost God

Discover how important your problems are to God's purposeful plan for your life, and how the RIGHT perspective makes all the difference!

Purchase today on Amazon.com!

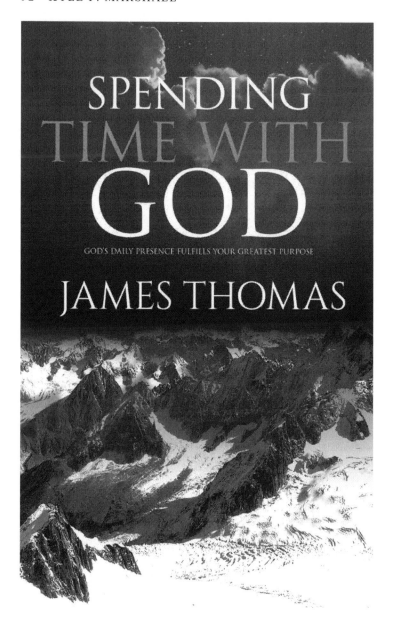

SPENDING
TIME WITH
GOD

GOD'S DAILY PRESENCE FULFILLS YOUR GREATEST PURPOSE

JAMES THOMAS

Spending time with God is one of the greatest privileges you have in life. Greater than your public worship, greater than your spiritual gifts, greater than preaching and teaching the gospel. When you commit yourself to spending time with your Heavenly Father on a daily basis, it will change your life. Period.

God wants to spend time with you, not because He's lonely, but because you so desperately need His daily presence in order to fulfill your greatest purpose.

In *Spending Time With God*, you'll learn super practical ways to draw near to your Heavenly Father and experience life-changing transformation as He draws near to you. For starters, you'll discover:

• 4 disciplines that motivate and inspire spending time with God

• The incredible impact of spending time with God

• Required elements for spending time with God

• The power of prayer and praise while spending time with God

Prepare yourself for the spectacular. Because when you experience God's daily presence, He fulfills your greatest purpose.

Purchase today on Amazon.com!

SCOTT SANDERS

HOLY
SPIRIT
TRAINING

DISCOVER THE PREDOMINANT
DIVINE POWER ON EARTH

If you've ever wondered if you've completely missed the purpose and ministry of the Holy Spirit, then this book might be a shocker for you.

There's a big difference between knowing the characteristics of the Spirit and knowing the Spirit as a person. The Holy Spirit is the predominant divine power on earth right now. But do you truly know Him?

In Holy Spirit Training, you'll train your senses to know there's more going on than what your eyes can see, discover how the Spirit is the key to accessing the "things" God has prepared for you, and learn exactly who the Spirit is and how He works. Get ready to discover:

• The role of the Holy Spirit in your life

• How to pick up the signals of the Holy Spirit

• How to follow and be led by the Holy Spirit

• How to partner with the Holy Spirit to manifest things on earth

Don't hesitate another day. Decide now to truly know the Holy Spirit and let Him guide you through life and put some *super* on your *natural*!

Purchase today on Amazon.com!

In the subtitle of this book, I chose the two themes of revelation and revolution because as I meditated on God loving me specifically and personally … it transformed my Christianity.

Like stated in Romans 12:2, my mind was renewed and my Christian walk revolutionized. It dawned on me that my sins alone put Jesus on that cross. Had the world not consisted of billions of people and instead the world only consisted of little ole me, He still would have had to die. My personal sin debt was enormous. I was born in sin and shaped in iniquity. There were no two ways around it. Yet, He did what He did because He loved me. Always had, and always will. He loves me.

It is for this revelation alone that I wrote this book: so that you too can be revolutionized, like I was and still am being because it's a journey you never exit. Or ever want to. So I invite you to join me in a discovery of revelation and revolution as God unveils what it means to be loved by the Creator of the universe!

Purchase today on Amazon.com!

Action Plan Template

Purpose: To create an action plan for accomplishing your mission to get to your vision.

Directions:
1. Using this form as a template, develop an action plan for each goal identified. *Modify the form as needed to fit your unique context.*
2. Distribute copies of each action plan to the those that you will collaborate to accomplish your goal.
3. Keep copies handy to bring to review and update regularly.

Goal:

Results/Accomplishments:

Action Steps *What Will Be Done?*	Responsibilities *Who Will Do It?*	Timeline *By When?* *(Day/Month)*	Resources A. *Resources Available* B. *Resources Needed (financial, human, political & other)*	Potential Barriers A. *What individuals or organizations might resist?* B. *How?*	Communications Plan *Who is involved?* *What methods?* *How often?*
Step 1:			A. B.	A. B.	
Step 2:			A. B.	A. B.	
Step 3:			A. B.	A. B.	
Step 4:			A. B.	A. B.	
Step 5:			A. B.	A. B.	

Evidence Of Success *(How will you know that you are making progress? What are your benchmarks?)*

Evaluation Process *(How will you determine that your goal has been reached? What are your measures?)*

Personal SWOT Analysis Template

You Are Fearfully and Wonderfully Made – What Do You Think GOD Put You On Earth To Do?

YOUR PURPOSE: _____

1 Write Down Your Purpose
2 Complete this SWOT Analysis
3 Take Action to
  a   Strengthen the Strengths
  b   Overcome the Weaknesses
  c   Leverage the Opportunities
  d   Defend Against Threats

strengths

Identify 3-5 examples

What do you do well?

What do you do better than others?

What competencies you possess to fulfil your purpose?

Essentially – WHAT AM I GREAT AT!

weaknesses

Identify 3-5 examples

What you do NOT do well?

What do others do better than you?

What skills that needs improvement in order to fulfil your purpose?

Essentially – WHAT DO I NEED TO WORK ON!

opportunities

Identify 3-5 examples

Do you see a place where you can do what you are called to do?

Do you see a need around you?

What things can you leverage to help you fulfil your purpose?

Essentially – WHAT AM I BEST SUITED FOR!

threats

Identify 3-5 examples

What personal/internal hindrances?

What are your social, financial, professional or other external hindrances?

What is/could hold you back from fulfilling your purpose?

Essentially – WHAT STANDS IN MY WAY OF SUCCESS